Math
Motivators

Grades 1–3

MORE GOOD YEAR BOOKS® IN MATHEMATICS

CRUISING INTO MEASUREMENTS: Over 40 Ready-to-Reproduce Activities and Games for Grades K–2 Runelle Konsler and Lauren Mirabella

DR. JIM'S ELEMENTARY MATH PRESCRIPTIONS: Grades 4–6   James L. Overholt

MATH ACTIVITIES WITH A PORPOISE: Over 45 Ready-to-Reproduce Activities and Games for Grades K–2   Runelle Konsler and Lauren Mirabella

MATH MOTIVATORS: Puzzles, Games, Bulletin Boards, and Special Motivators, Grades 4–6 Marian R. Bartch and Jerry J. Mallett

MEASUREMENT AND THE CHILD'S ENVIRONMENT: Grades K–6   Tamara J. Keyser and Randall J. Souviney

THE PRIMARY MATH LAB: An Active Learning Approach, Grades 1–3   Shirley S. Price and Merle E. Price

SOLVING PROBLEMS KIDS CARE ABOUT: Math Skills and Word Problems, Grades 4–8 Randall J. Souviney

For information about these or any Good Year Books®, please contact your local school supply store or

Good Year Books
Scott, Foresman and Company
1900 East Lake Avenue
Glenview, Illinois 60025

Grades 1–3

Math Motivators

PUZZLES, GAMES, BULLETIN BOARDS, AND SPECIAL MOTIVATORS

Marian R. Bartch
Jerry J. Mallett

Scott, Foresman and Company
Glenview, Illinois   London

ISBN 0-673-18264-9

About This Book

Mathematical drill and practice exercises are often described as "dull," "boring," or "the same old thing" by both students and teachers. Such exercises are, however, essential for mastering the basic facts of every arithmetical operation. The function of this book is to provide teachers with a wide variety of activities and games to spark and maintain students' interest in skills-work practice. The material is divided into five sections for easy selection of appropriate activities.

I Games for Individual Instruction
II Games for Group Instruction
III Puzzle Sheets
IV Learning Boards
V Special Motivators

Each game or activity is arranged in mathematical sequence—from the basic foundation skills to more advanced operations. Each focuses on a specific skill and is keyed to an approximate grade level. Detailed directions for construction and use are provided to ensure quick and easy adaptation for any classroom.

Moreover, the accompanying patterns of game components can be copied and used immediately. Also included is a skills listing, which classifies each game or activity under a specific skills heading.

Most of the puzzle pages are self-correcting and can be duplicated just as they are. The learning boards may be easily reproduced by using an opaque projector. All materials needed for the games and activities are readily available, making this book an accessible and convenient teaching aid.

By using the materials in this book as supplementary exercises in the classroom mathematics program, teachers will keep their students' interest and motivation high as well as enable them to master important and necessary mathematical skills. The wide range of skills and grade-level suitability permit a more individualized approach for teachers who strive to meet the unique needs and abilities of each student.

The authors wish to thank Carol George and Anne Cernak for their helpful reviews.

Contents

Mathematical Skills

PART I

Games for Individual Instruction

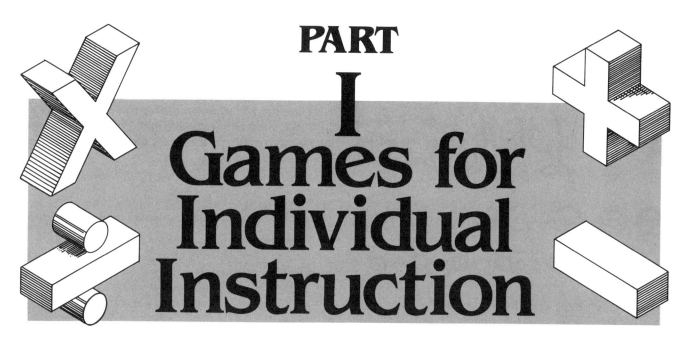

Mathematics learning requires an emphasis upon drill and practice exercises that reinforce or maintain the initial instruction. These exercises, though necessarily repetitious, need not be "boring" if they are varied through the use of games and other creative activities. Concept understanding and skills mastery vary greatly among students in any given classroom. Individualization of instruction and pacing of learning can be achieved by using self-checking games. The games' built-in self-checks allow students to receive immediate feedback and strengthen their grasp of mathematical principles. This feedback also tells teachers whether more practice is needed in certain concept areas.

The individualized, self-check games in this section are easy to make, for construction details are clearly described. The materials used in most of the games—posterboard, color markers, scissors, glue—are readily available to the classroom teacher. Other materials are inexpensive and easy to collect.

The games are arranged in mathematical sequence from the easiest skills to the more difficult.

Help Choo Choo Find His Coal Car

Skill Reinforced: One-to-one correspondence/ Equivalent sets

Materials Needed:
- 10 sheets of 4″ × 5″ gray posterboard
- scissors
- felt-tipped pen
- color markers or stars

Construction Directions:
1. Cut five of the posterboard pieces using the engine pattern shown here.

2. Mark each of the following groups of objects on a different engine shape in the manner shown in the illustration.

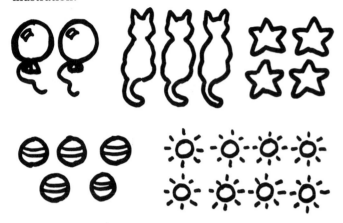

3. Cut and mark the other five posterboard pieces using the coal-car pattern shown here.

4. Mark each of the following groups of objects on a different coal car in the manner shown in the illustration. On the backs of the pieces with the objects drawn on them, place a corresponding number of markers or stars in the same color.

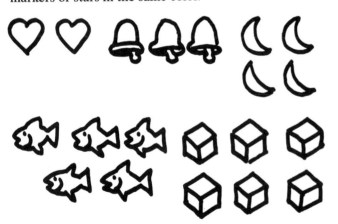

Game Play:
1. Find one of the engines and place it on your desk.
2. How many objects are on this engine? Now look through all the coal cars and see if you can find one with the same number of objects.
3. When you find it, place it in back of the engine.
4. Do this with all the engines and coal cars. When you are finished, turn over the pieces for the self-check. The colors should be the same.

My Dog Spot

Skill Reinforced: Inequalities

Materials Needed:
- 1 sheet of 5″ × 8″ white posterboard
- 10 sheets of 3″ × 5″ white posterboard
- scissors
- felt-tipped pen

Construction Directions:
1. Cut and mark the large posterboard piece using an enlargement of the dog pattern shown here.

2. Cut and mark the small posterboard pieces using the same dog pattern. Do not mark the spots on the dogs.
3. Now mark the following number of spots on the dogs as indicated:

> one spot on two dogs
> two spots on two dogs
> three spots on two dogs
> four spots on two dogs
> five spots on two dogs

4. Mark a smile face on the backs of the dogs with four and five spots.

Game Play:

1. Place the large dog in front of you. How many spots are on this dog? That's right, three.

2. Look at one of the small dogs. Does it have more spots than the large dog? If it does, place it under the large dog. Do the same with the rest of the dogs.

3. When you are finished, turn the dogs over. If you've done it right, all the dogs you placed under the large dog should have smile faces on them.

Hey Diddle Diddle

Skill Reinforced: Counting

Materials Needed:
- 5 sheets of 5″ × 6″ white posterboard
- 5 sheets of 3″ × 4″ tan posterboard
- scissors
- felt-tipped pens in various colors
- color markers or stars

Construction Directions:

1. Cut and mark the white posterboard pieces using the cat pattern shown here.

2. On each cat, print a different number from 1 through 5, as shown in the illustration.

3. Cut and mark the tan posterboard pieces using the fiddle pattern shown here.

4. On each fiddle, draw a different number of strings beginning with one string on the first fiddle and ending with five on the last one.

5. Place corresponding color markers on the backs of the playing pieces so that they are self-checking.

Game Play:

1. Place the cats in one pile and the fiddles in another.

2. Look at one of the fiddles. How many strings does it have?

3. Look through the cats and see if you can find that numeral. If you find it, place that cat on the fiddle.

4. Do the same with the rest of the pieces.

5. When you are finished, turn over the pieces and see if you are right. The color markers should be the same.

Sally Sea Serpent

Skill Reinforced: Sequence/Counting

Materials Needed:
- 1 sheet of 5″ × 14″ white posterboard
- felt-tipped pens in various colors
- scissors

Construction Directions:

1. Mark and cut the posterboard using an enlargement of the sea serpent pattern shown here. Cut on the dotted lines.

Game Play:

1. Place the game pieces in front of you.

2. Now put the parts of Sally's body together in the correct numerical order.

Fido Has the Answer

Skill Reinforced: Single-digit addends/No regrouping/Commutative property

Materials Needed:
- 10 sheets of 5″ × 7″ red posterboard
- 10 sheets of 2″ × 6″ white posterboard
- felt-tipped pens in various colors
- scissors

Construction Directions:
1. Cut and mark the red posterboard pieces using the doghouse pattern shown here.

2. Cut and mark the white posterboard pieces using the dog pattern shown here.

3. On each doghouse, print one of the following problems in the manner shown in the illustration. On each dog strip, print one of the following answer sets (indicated in parentheses) as shown in the illustration. Slide the dog strip through the slit in the doghouse.

$$3 + 2 = (5 \quad 6 \quad 4) \qquad 3 + 3 = (5 \quad 6 \quad 7)$$
$$3 + 5 = (7 \quad 8 \quad 6) \qquad 3 + 6 = (7 \quad 8 \quad 9)$$
$$4 + 2 = (5 \quad 7 \quad 6) \qquad 4 + 3 = (7 \quad 6 \quad 8)$$
$$4 + 5 = (9 \quad 8 \quad 7) \qquad 5 + 2 = (6 \quad 7 \quad 8)$$
$$3 + 4 = (6 \quad 7 \quad 8) \qquad 6 + 2 = (7 \quad 8 \quad 9)$$

4. Mark the correct answer on the back of each doghouse.

Game Play:
1. Look at the problem on one of the doghouses.
2. Pull out Fido and find the correct answer. When you think you have found it, turn over the game piece to see whether you are right.
3. Do this with all the game pieces.

Baby Birds

Skill Reinforced: Double-digit addends/No regrouping

Materials Needed:
■ 10 sheets of 6″ × 8″ white posterboard
■ 20 sheets of 1″ × 3″ white posterboard
■ scissors
■ felt-tipped pens in various colors

Construction Directions:
1. Mark and cut two $1\frac{1}{2}$″ slits in the large white posterboard pieces using an enlargement of the pattern shown here.

2. Cut and mark the small posterboard pieces using the baby bird pattern shown here.

3. Slide a baby bird into each slit in the gameboards.
4. On each gameboard, copy a different one of the following problems in the manner shown in the illustration. On each baby bird, print one of the following answers (indicated in parentheses) as shown in the illustration. Pull the baby birds up and mark

each one either "Correct" or "Incorrect" depending on its answer.

$$12 + 12 = (24 \quad 26) \qquad 13 + 14 = (27 \quad 29)$$
$$24 + 12 = (36 \quad 39) \qquad 25 + 11 = (36 \quad 37)$$
$$11 + 11 = (22 \quad 21) \qquad 36 + 21 = (57 \quad 55)$$
$$41 + 26 = (67 \quad 65) \qquad 24 + 13 = (37 \quad 35)$$
$$31 + 18 = (49 \quad 47) \qquad 27 + 11 = (38 \quad 39)$$

Game Play:
1. Look at one of the gameboards. You will see a problem on the mother bird. Which of the baby birds has the correct answer?
2. When you think you know, pull up that bird for the self-check. If you're right, you will see the word "Correct."

Drusilla the Dragon

Skill Reinforced: Three-digit addend and one-digit addend/No regrouping

Materials Needed:
- 10 sheets of 5″ × 8″ white posterboard
- 10 circles of white posterboard with 4″ diameters
- scissors
- felt-tipped pens in various colors
- 10 paper fasteners

Construction Directions:
1. Mark and cut the large posterboard pieces using an enlargement of the pattern shown here.

ATTACH FOOT
WHEEL WITH
PAPER FASTENER

2. Cut the posterboard circles using the foot wheel pattern shown here.

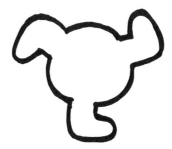

3. Fasten a foot wheel to each game piece in the manner shown in the illustration.
4. Copy each of the following problems on a different gameboard, marking each foot with one of the three answer choices shown under the problem. Mark the correct answer on the back of each gameboard.

$$
\begin{array}{ll}
215 & 374 \\
+\ \ 4 & +\ \ 4 \\
\hline
218 \quad 219 \quad 220 & 377 \quad 379 \quad 378 \\
\end{array}
$$

$$
\begin{array}{ll}
162 & 475 \\
+\ \ 6 & +\ \ 3 \\
\hline
166 \quad 167 \quad 168 & 478 \quad 477 \quad 479 \\
\end{array}
$$

$$
\begin{array}{ll}
543 & 582 \\
+\ \ 5 & +\ \ 3 \\
\hline
548 \quad 547 \quad 549 & 584 \quad 585 \quad 586 \\
\end{array}
$$

$$
\begin{array}{ll}
691 & 731 \\
+\ \ 8 & +\ \ 7 \\
\hline
698 \quad 699 \quad 700 & 737 \quad 738 \quad 739 \\
\end{array}
$$

$$
\begin{array}{ll}
882 & 944 \\
+\ \ 1 & +\ \ 2 \\
\hline
884 \quad 885 \quad 883 & 945 \quad 946 \quad 947 \\
\end{array}
$$

Game Play:
1. Look at one of the gameboards. The answer to the problem is on one of Drusilla's feet. Turn the wheel and see if you can find it.
2. When you think you have found the correct answer, turn over the gameboard and see if you are right.

Gas Up the Car

Skill Reinforced: Double-digit addends/Regrouping

Materials Needed:
- 10 sheets of 3″ × 5″ posterboard in various colors
- 10 sheets of 2½″ × 6″ red posterboard
- 10 shoelaces
- scissors
- felt-tipped pen
- paper hole punch
- tape

Construction Directions:

1. Cut, mark, and punch a hole in the 3″ × 5″ posterboard pieces using the car pattern shown here.

2. Print each of the following answers on a different car in the manner shown in the illustration. On the back of each car, mark the corresponding circled numeral. Be sure to circle it.

42 ①		61 ②	
91 ③		95 ④	
51 ⑤		94 ⑥	
92 ⑦		71 ⑧	
40 ⑨		90 ⑩	

3. Cut, mark, and punch a hole in the red posterboard pieces as shown here. Attach the shoelaces by putting them through the holes and taping them to the back.

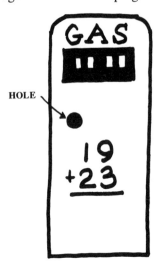

4. Copy each of the following problems on a different gas pump in the manner shown in the illustration. Mark the corresponding circled numeral on the back of each pump. Be sure to circle it.

19 ① +23		27 ② +34
72 ③ +19		66 ④ +29
25 ⑤ +26		38 ⑥ +56
63 ⑦ +29		49 ⑧ +22
12 ⑨ +28		15 ⑩ +75

Game Play:

1. Place the cars face up in one pile and the gas pumps in another.

2. Look at the problem on one of the gas pumps. Do you know the answer? Look for the car that has the correct answer written on it.

3. When you think you have found it, place the gas pump's hose in the hole in the car and go on to the next gas pump. Do this with all the pieces.

4. When you are finished, you may turn over the pieces for the self-check. The circled numerals should be the same for each pair.

Help Claude Find His Tail!

Skill Reinforced: Subtracting multiples of 10/No regrouping/Double-digit subtrahend and double-digit minuend

Materials Needed:
- 9 sheets of 5″ × 6″ white posterboard
- scissors
- felt-tipped pen (brown)
- color markers or stars

Construction Directions:
1. Cut and mark the posterboard pieces using the cat pattern shown below. Be sure to cut off the tails on the dotted lines.

COLOR SPOTS BROWN

2. Copy the following problems on the cats' bodies and answers on their tails, as shown in the illustration. Place the same-color markers on the backs of the problems and answers that go together.

$$\begin{array}{ccccc} 30 & 90 & 70 & 70 & 80 \\ -20 & -70 & -40 & -30 & -20 \\ \hline 10 & 20 & 30 & 40 & 60 \end{array}$$

$$\begin{array}{cccc} 80 & 90 & 10 & 70 \\ -10 & -10 & -10 & -20 \\ \hline 70 & 80 & 0 & 50 \end{array}$$

Game Play:
1. Place the cats in one pile and tails in another.
2. Look at the problem on one of the cats. Do you know the answer? Look through the tails and see if you can find the answer. When you think you have found it, place it on the cat. Now do the same with the rest of the pieces.

3. When you are finished, turn over the pieces for the self-check. The color markers should be the same on each pair.

Laughing Lollipops

Skill Reinforced: Double-digit subtrahend and double-digit minuend/No regrouping

Materials Needed:
- 10 posterboard circles of various colors with 4″ diameters
- 10 popsicle sticks
- glue
- felt-tipped pen

Construction Directions:
1. Mark the circles and then glue them onto the popsicle sticks using the pattern shown here.

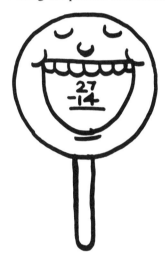

2. Print each of the following problems on a different lollipop in the manner shown in the illustration. Copy the corresponding answers on the backs.

$$\begin{array}{ccccc} 27 & 34 & 49 & 57 & 69 \\ -14 & -11 & -43 & -55 & -19 \\ \hline 13 & 23 & 6 & 2 & 50 \end{array}$$

$$\begin{array}{ccccc} 77 & 88 & 91 & 54 & 75 \\ -52 & -18 & -21 & -21 & -22 \\ \hline 25 & 70 & 70 & 33 & 53 \end{array}$$

Game Play:
1. Look at the problem on one of the laughing lollipops. Do you know what the answer is? Try to figure it out.
2. When you think you know, turn it over and see if you are correct.
3. Do this with all the lollipops.

Put On Your Boots

Skill Reinforced: Single-digit multiplicand and single-digit multiplier/Communicative property/Basic facts

Materials Needed:
- 3 sheets of 6″ × 10″ tan posterboard
- paper hole punch
- felt-tipped pens in various colors
- 4 shoelaces each in a different color

Construction Directions:
1. Cut, mark, and punch holes into the posterboard pieces using an enlargement of the boot pattern shown here.

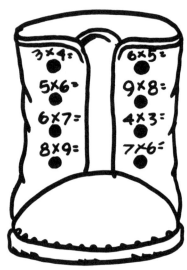

2. Print the following problems on the boots in two columns, as shown in the illustration. On the reverse side, surround the holes of corresponding problems with the same-color felt-tipped pen.

Boot #1
3 × 4 =	6 × 5 =
5 × 6 =	9 × 8 =
6 × 7 =	4 × 3 =
8 × 9 =	7 × 6 =

Boot #2
2 × 5 =	3 × 6 =
6 × 3 =	8 × 9 =
7 × 8 =	8 × 7 =
9 × 8 =	5 × 2 =

Boot #3
5 × 4 =	4 × 9 =
9 × 3 =	4 × 5 =
4 × 7 =	3 × 9 =
9 × 4 =	7 × 4 =

Game Play:
1. Take one of the boots and all four shoelaces.
2. Place a shoelace in the hole under one of the problems. Now look down the problems in the other column. Can you find a problem that has the same answer? Put the other end of the shoelace in the hole under that problem. Do the same with the rest of the problems.
3. When you are finished, turn the boot over. Check to see whether your answers are right by seeing if the same shoelace is in both holes of the same color.

Silly Silos

Skill Reinforced: Double-digit multiplicand and single-digit multiplier/Multiples of 10/Basic facts/Zero in multiplication

Materials Needed:
- 10 sheets of 6″ × 8″ red posterboard
- 10 sheets of 3″ × 9″ red posterboard
- scissors
- felt-tipped pen

Construction Directions:
1. Cut and mark the large posterboard pieces using an enlargement of the barn pattern shown here.

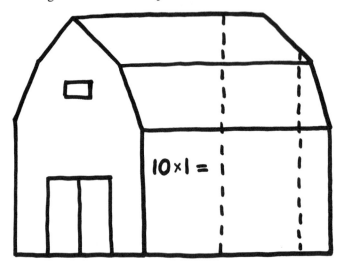

From *Math Motivators*, Copyright © 1986 Scott, Foresman and Company

2. Cut and mark the small posterboard pieces using an enlargement of the silo pattern shown here.

3. Copy the following problems and answers on the game pieces in the manner shown in the illustrations.

$10 \times 0 = 0$	$10 \times 1 = 10$
$10 \times 2 = 20$	$10 \times 3 = 30$
$10 \times 4 = 40$	$10 \times 5 = 50$
$10 \times 6 = 60$	$10 \times 7 = 70$
$10 \times 8 = 80$	$10 \times 9 = 90$

4. Be sure to copy the correct answer on the back of each barn for the self-check.

Game Play:
1. Place the barns in one pile and the silos in another.
2. Look at the problem on one of the barns. Do you know the answer? Look through all the silos and see if you can find it.
3. When you think you have found it, place that silo on the barn. Do the same with all the game pieces.
4. When you are finished, turn the game pieces over for the self-check.

Piglet's Problems

Skill Reinforced: Double-digit multiplicand and single-digit multiplier/No regrouping/Identity element/Zero in multiplication

Materials Needed:
■ 7 sheets of 6″ × 10″ pink posterboard
■ 7 shoelaces
■ scissors
■ paper hole punch
■ tape
■ felt-tipped pen

Construction Directions:
1. Cut, mark, and punch holes in the posterboard pieces using an enlargement of the pig pattern shown here.

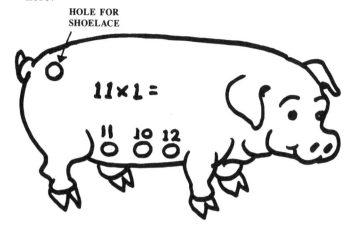

2. Copy each of the following problems and alternative answer sets onto different pigs in the manner shown in the illustration.

$11 \times 1 =$		
11	10	12
$16 \times 1 =$		
17	15	16
$36 \times 0 =$		
1	36	0
$98 \times 0 =$		
98	198	0

$15 \times 1 =$		
14	15	16
$75 \times 0 =$		
0	75	74
$62 \times 0 =$		
0	62	162

3. Mark around the backside of the hole that is under the correct answer.
4. Put the end of a shoelace through the hole in the pig's tail and attach it to the backside with tape.

Game Play:
1. Look at the problem on one of the pigs.
2. Do you know the answer? It is on this pig. When you think you know which it is, place the shoelace through the hole that is under the correct answer.
3. Now turn the pig over for the self-check. The shoelace should be through the hole that is marked.

A Whale of a "Tail"

Skill Reinforced: Single-digit divisor and double-digit dividend/No regrouping/No remainders

Materials Needed:
■ 10 sheets of 4″ × 9″ white posterboard
■ scissors
■ felt-tipped pens in various colors

Construction Directions:
1. Cut, mark, and fold the posterboard pieces using the pattern shown here.

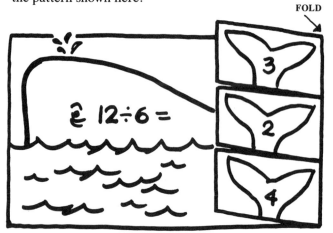

2. Copy each of the following problems along with the corresponding answers onto different game cards in the manner shown in the illustration. Mark a smile face under the flap containing the correct answer.

$$12 \div 6 = \begin{matrix} 3 \\ 2 \\ 4 \end{matrix} \qquad 12 \div 2 = \begin{matrix} 6 \\ 5 \\ 4 \end{matrix} \qquad 10 \div 5 = \begin{matrix} 4 \\ 3 \\ 2 \end{matrix}$$

$$10 \div 2 = \begin{matrix} 4 \\ 5 \\ 6 \end{matrix} \qquad 14 \div 7 = \begin{matrix} 3 \\ 2 \\ 5 \end{matrix} \qquad 14 \div 2 = \begin{matrix} 7 \\ 5 \\ 6 \end{matrix}$$

$$16 \div 2 = \begin{matrix} 7 \\ 9 \\ 8 \end{matrix} \qquad 16 \div 8 = \begin{matrix} 4 \\ 3 \\ 2 \end{matrix} \qquad 20 \div 2 = \begin{matrix} 12 \\ 10 \\ 8 \end{matrix}$$

$$18 \div 2 = \begin{matrix} 8 \\ 9 \\ 7 \end{matrix}$$

Game Play:
1. Take one of the gameboards and look at the problem on the whale. Do you know the answer? The correct answer is on one of the whale's tails.
2. When you think you know the answer, lift up that tail. If you see a smile face you are correct.

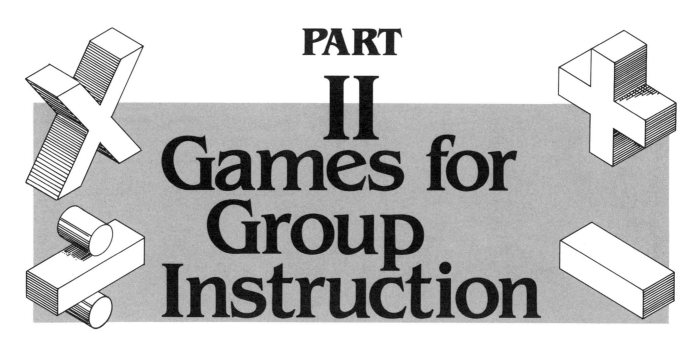

PART II
Games for Group Instruction

Participation in mathematics games and activities, in both large and small groups, promotes the acquisition of skills and concepts and provides motivation to learn. Additionally, games offer the kind of variety that makes drill and practice an enjoyable experience instead of one that is rather routine and dull.

The use of group games in mathematics instruction provides a beneficial exchange of ideas and a sharing of learning among students of all ability levels. The game method of reinforcement keeps students of high ability from becoming bored with "the same old worksheets," it reinforces students of average ability, and it encourages students of lesser ability to keep trying to achieve. Moreover, teachers can utilize mathematics game-playing as a diagnostic tool to determine the need for either challenge or remediation among students.

The group games, like the individual games, are easy to make, and each includes clear construction directions and a list of needed materials. The games are arranged in mathematical sequence from the easiest skills to the more difficult.

Fill the Aquarium

Skill Reinforced: One-to-one correspondence

Materials Needed:
- 6 sheets of 9″ × 7″ blue posterboard
- 18 sheets of 2″ × 2″ orange posterboard
- felt-tipped pen
- scissors
- glue

Construction Directions:
1. Cut and mark the orange posterboard pieces using the fish pattern shown here.

2. Copy each of the following dot combinations on three different fish in the manner shown in the illustration.

3. Cut and mark the blue posterboard pieces using the aquarium pattern shown here. To each aquarium glue a fish with a different combination of dots. Place the remaining fish in a pile.

Game Play: This game can be played by two to six players.

1. Each player chooses an aquarium gameboard. The fish are placed in the center of the playing area so that all the players can see the marks on them.

2. Explain that two fish are missing from each aquarium. All the missing fish can be found in the pile in the center of the playing area. Each child must find two fish that match the fish glued onto his or her aquarium.

3. The first player chooses a fish and puts it in her aquarium. If it is the correct fish, she keeps it. If the fish does not match, the player must put it back in the pile. The next player continues the game in the same manner. The first player to put his fish in his aquarium is the winner.

Quiet Quackers

Skill Reinforced: Sequence

Materials Needed:
■ 4 sheets of 5″ × 16″ yellow posterboard
■ 16 sheets of 3″ × 3″ yellow posterboard
■ scissors
■ felt-tipped pen

Construction Directions:

1. Cut and mark the four large posterboard pieces using an enlargement of the pattern shown here.

2. Copy each of the numeral pairs onto a different gameboard in the manner shown in the illustration.

1, 6
6, 11
11, 16
16, 21

3. Cut the smaller posterboard pieces using the duck pattern shown below.

4. Copy each of the following numerals on a different duck in the manner shown in the illustration.

2, 3, 4, 5, 7, 8, 9, 10, 12, 13, 14, 15, 17, 18, 19, 20

Game Play: This game is for two to four players.

1. Each player chooses a gameboard strip and places it in front of him.

2. All the ducks are dealt, face down, to the players. The children should not be able to see the numerals on each other's ducks.

3. Players now look at the ducks in their hands. If they have any that can be placed in correct numerical sequence between the two ducks on their gameboard, they should put these in the appropriate slots.

4. The player who dealt the ducks now begins the game by holding out the ducks in his hand, face down, to the player on his left. This player must take one of the ducks. She must not show the numeral to any other player. If it fits in the correct numerical sequence on her gameboard, she places it in the appropriate slot. If not, she adds it to the ducks in her hand and continues the game by holding out her ducks, face down, to the player on her left.

5. The game continues in this manner until one of the players fills in all the slots on his gameboard. This player is the winner.

Loop the Life-Saver

Skill Reinforced: Equivalent sets

Materials Needed:
- 5 sheets of 7″ × 7″ heavy corrugated cardboard
- 5 cardboard 5″ paper rolls
- 1 sheet of 6″ × 6″ red posterboard
- 20 sheets of 3″ × 3″ white posterboard
- felt-tipped pen
- tape
- scissors

Construction Directions:
1. Tape each cardboard roll to a different corrugated cardboard sheet as shown here.

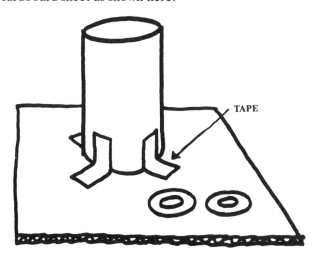

2. Copy each of the following life-saver groups onto a different game piece in the manner shown in the illustration.

3. Cut the red posterboard piece using an enlargement of the life-saver pattern shown here.

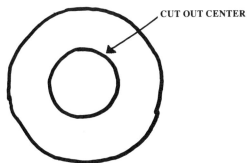

4. Copy each of the following groups onto a different white posterboard piece.

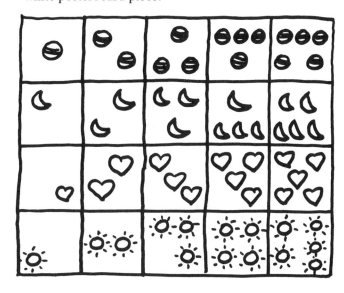

Game Play: This game can be played with two to five players.
1. The players sit in a semicircle with the gameboards placed approximately four feet in front of them. The 20 picture cards are placed on the floor, picture side up, between the players and the boards.
2. The player on the left goes first. This player takes the life-saver and attempts to toss it over the roll on any one of the boards. If he fails, the life-saver goes to the next player. If this player succeeds, she is entitled to find a picture card that has the same number of life-savers as the ringed gameboard. If she is correct, she can keep the card. If she makes a mistake in choosing a card, she puts the incorrect card back on the floor. Either way, the next player takes his turn.
3. The game is over when the last picture card has been picked up. The winner is the player who has collected the most picture cards.

Peter Penguin's Problems

Skill Reinforced: Single-digit addends/Commutative property/Basic facts

Materials Needed:
- 18 sheets of 3″ × 4″ white posterboard
- 6 sheets of 9″ × 9″ white posterboard
- felt-tipped pen
- scissors

Construction Directions:
1. Cut and mark the small posterboard pieces using the penguin pattern shown here.

2. Copy each of the following problems onto a different penguin in the manner shown in the illustration.

2 + 2 =	3 + 2 =	3 + 3 =
4 + 3 =	1 + 3 =	1 + 4 =
4 + 2 =	2 + 5 =	3 + 1 =
2 + 3 =	1 + 5 =	6 + 1 =
4 + 4 =	5 + 4 =	5 + 3 =
7 + 2 =	2 + 6 =	1 + 8 =

3. Cut and mark the large posterboard pieces using an enlargement of the igloo pattern shown here.

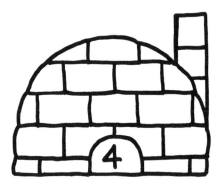

4. Copy each of the following numerals onto a different igloo as shown in the illustration.

4, 5, 6, 7, 8, 9

Game Play: This game can be played by two to six players.
1. Each player chooses an igloo. The penguins are placed in the center of the playing area so that all the players can see the problems on them.
2. Explain that three penguins are missing from each igloo. Each child must find the three penguins whose problems produce the answer on his or her igloo.
3. The first player chooses a penguin and puts it on his igloo. If it is the correct penguin, he keeps it. If the penguin does not have a correct problem, the player must put the penguin back in the pile. The next player continues the game in the same manner. The first player to have all three penguins on her igloo is the winner.

UFOs

Skill Reinforced: Single-digit multiplicant and single-digit multiplier/No regrouping

Materials Needed:
- 3 sheets of 12″ × 12″ light blue posterboard
- 12 sheets of 3″ × 4″ yellow posterboard
- scissors
- felt-tipped pen

Construction Directions:
1. Mark and cut four 3″ slits in the three blue posterboard pieces, using an enlargement of the gameboard pattern shown here.

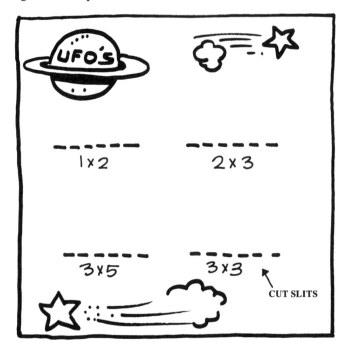

From *Math Motivators*, Copyright © 1986 Scott, Foresman and Company

2. Copy one of the problem groups onto each gameboard as shown in the illustration.

Group 1	*Group 2*	*Group 3*
1 × 2 =	1 × 3 =	2 × 2 =
2 × 3 =	2 × 4 =	1 × 5 =
3 × 5 =	4 × 5 =	3 × 4 =
3 × 3 =	1 × 1 =	2 × 5 =

3. Cut and mark the small yellow posterboard pieces using the UFO pattern shown here.

4. Copy each of the following answers onto a different UFO as shown in the illustration.

2, 6, 15, 9, 3, 8, 20, 1, 4, 5, 12, 10

Game Play: This game is for two or three players.
1. Each player chooses a gameboard. The UFOs are placed face down in the center of the playing area.
2. The first player takes a UFO and looks at the numeral. If this in an answer for one of the problems on his gameboard, he slips it through the slit above the appropriate problem. If it is not a correct answer, he places the UFO on the bottom of the stack from which it came.
3. The next player continues the game in the same manner.
4. The first player to place four UFOs correctly on her gameboard is the winner.

Hickory Dickory Dock

Skill Reinforced: Single-digit addends/Fact families/ Basic facts

Materials Needed:
- 1 sheet of 8″ × 8″ white posterboard
- 24 sheets of 2½″ × 3″ gray posterboard
- scissors
- paper hole punch
- felt-tipped pen
- spinner from an old game

Construction Directions:
1. Mark and cut the white posterboard piece using the clock pattern shown here. Attach it to the spinner as shown.

2. Mark the gray posterboard pieces using the pattern shown here.

3. Copy each of the following problems onto a different mouse card as shown in the illustration.

6	7	8	9	8
+6	+5	+4	+3	+7
9	7	6	5	6
+6	+8	+9	+5	+4
7	8	7	8	9
+3	+2	+7	+6	+7
6	5	4	3	9
+8	+6	+7	+8	+2
9	8	6	5	
+4	+5	+7	+8	

Game Play: This game can be played by two to four players.

1. Spread the mouse cards face down in the center of the playing area.

2. The first player spins the clock. When the spinner stops, the player turns over one of the cards. If the card has a problem whose answer the spinner stopped on, the player may keep the mouse. If not, he returns the card, face down, to the playing area.

3. The player to his left continues the game in the same manner.

4. When all the mouse cards have been collected, the game is finished. The player with the most cards wins.

Never-Never Land

Skill Reinforced: Double-digit addends/No regrouping

Materials Needed:
- 1 sheet of 24″ × 24″ white posterboard
- 30 sheets of 2½″ × 3″ red posterboard
- 6 game markers
- felt-tipped pens in various colors

Construction Directions:

1. Mark the large posterboard piece using an enlargement of the gameboard pattern shown here.

2. Copy each of the following sets of problems and directions on a different red card.

$14 + 21 =$
Move ahead one space.

$41 + 18 =$
Move ahead two spaces.

$26 + 31 =$
Move ahead three spaces.

$52 + 22 =$
Move ahead one space.

$15 + 13 =$
Move ahead two spaces.

$21 + 35 =$
Move ahead three spaces.

$36 + 52 =$
Move ahead one space.

$81 + 15 =$
Move ahead two spaces.

$65 + 22 =$
Move ahead three spaces.

$46 + 11 =$
Move ahead one space.

$41 + 36 =$
Move ahead two spaces.

$14 + 71 =$
Move ahead three spaces.

$18 + 61 =$
Move ahead one space.

$82 + 15 =$
Move ahead two spaces.

$65 + 13 =$
Move ahead three spaces.

$58 + 31 =$
Move ahead one space.

$36 + 33 =$
Move ahead two spaces.

$24 + 24 =$
Move ahead three spaces.

$18 + 11 =$
Move ahead one space.

$61 + 15 =$
Move ahead two spaces.

43 + 44 =
Move ahead three spaces.

72 + 15 =
Move ahead one space.

75 + 21 =
Move ahead two spaces.

33 + 33 =
Move ahead three spaces.

41 + 41 =
Move ahead one space.

Unicorn in path.
Lose a turn.

Dragon stops you.
Go back two spaces.

It is getting dark.
Go back three spaces.

You have lost your way.
Go back one space.

Herd of unicorn coming at you.
Go back three spaces.

Game Play: This game may be played by two to six players.
1. The gameboard is placed on a flat surface in the center of the group of players. All the cards should be shuffled and then stacked face down on the board where indicated. Each player chooses a marker and places it on START.
2. The first player takes the top card and reads the problem aloud. If he can correctly give the answer, he follows the directions to move ahead. If he is incorrect, he places the card face down on the bottom of the stack and the next player takes her turn. *Note:* A few cards are "penalty cards." When these are picked, the player simply follows the directions on the card.
3. The first player to reach "Stop" is the winner.

Tricky Tubs

Skill Reinforced: Double-digit addends/Regrouping

Materials Needed:
- 5 large margarine tubs and lids
- 20 sheets of $1\frac{1}{2}'' \times 2''$ white posterboard
- Con-Tact paper
- scissors
- felt-tipped pen

Construction Directions:
1. Cover the lids of the five tubs with Con-Tact paper and cut a 2″ slit in each.
2. Copy each of the following answers on a different lid.

53, 62, 74, 55, 76

3. Copy each of the following problems on a different card.

38	27	19	16	36
+15	+26	+34	+37	+26
15	43	28	47	36
+47	+19	+34	+27	+38
55	29	26	17	28
+19	+45	+29	+38	+27
16	47	38	39	17
+39	+29	+38	+37	+59

Game Play: This game may be played by two to five players.
1. Each player chooses a tub and places it in front of him.
2. All the problem cards are dealt to the players face down. A player should not show the other players his cards.
3. The players should now look at the cards in their hands. Those who hold a card whose problem produces the answer on their tub should slide the card through the slit and into the tub.
4. The player who dealt the cards now begins the game by holding out the cards in his hand, face down, to the player on his left. This player must take one of the cards and not show the card to any other player. If the problem matches the answer on her tub, she puts it in her tub. If not, she simply adds it to the cards in her hand and continues the game by holding out her cards to the player on her left.
5. The game is over when one of the players has been able to place four cards in his tub. This player is the winner.

Farmer Hank's Hen Yard

Skill Reinforced: Single-digit subtrahend/No regrouping/Basic facts

Materials Needed:
- 3 one-gallon cardboard milk containers
- 15 sheets of $1\frac{1}{2}'' \times 1\frac{1}{2}''$ red posterboard
- 3 long shoelaces
- spinner from an old game
- 3 sheets of green, yellow, and tan Con-Tact paper
- paper hole punch
- scissors
- felt-tipped pen
- tape

Construction Directions:
1. Cut and mount the Con-Tact paper onto the game spinner in the manner shown here.

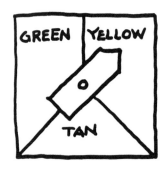

2. Cut the milk containers and cover each with a different color Con-Tact paper using the pattern shown one below.

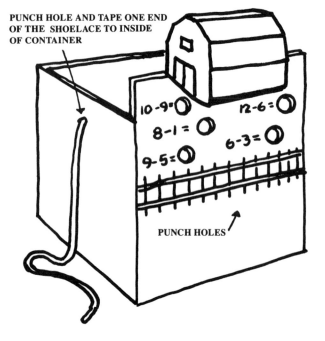

PUNCH HOLE AND TAPE ONE END OF THE SHOELACE TO INSIDE OF CONTAINER

PUNCH HOLES

3. Mark, punch holes, and attach a shoelace to each of the game boxes as shown in the illustration.
4. Mark and punch a hole in each of the red posterboard pieces using the hen pattern shown here.

5. Copy each of the following problem groups onto a different henyard gameboard as shown in the illustration.

Group 1	*Group 2*	*Group 3*
10 − 9 =	10 − 8 =	10 − 7 =
9 − 5 =	9 − 4 =	9 − 3 =
8 − 1 =	11 − 3 =	12 − 3 =
6 − 3 =	5 − 1 =	10 − 5 =
12 − 6 =	11 − 4 =	10 − 2 =

6. Copy each of the following numerals on a different hen as shown in the illustration.

1, 4, 7, 3, 6, 2, 5, 8, 4, 7, 3, 6, 9, 5, 8

Game Play: This game is for three players.
1. Each player places a henyard in front of him. The hens are spread out, numeral side up, in the center of the playing area.
2. The players take turns spinning the arrow. When the spinner stops on a color, the player who has the same color henyard looks for a hen with the correct answer to one of her henyard problems. She then "sews" it to the hole under the appropriate problem.
3. Players continue to "sew" the answers to the problems on their gameboards as their color comes up on the spinner.
4. The first player to correctly "sew" all five hens to her henyard is the winner.

Candy Store

Skill Reinforced: Single-digit subtrahend and double-digit minuend/Regrouping

Materials Needed:
- 3 sheets of 9″ × 12″ white posterboard
- 15 sheets of 3″ × 4″ white posterboard
- felt-tipped pens in various colors
- scissors
- spinner from an old game
- 1 sheet of red construction paper
- 1 sheet of green construction paper
- glue

Construction Directions:

1. Mark the large posterboard pieces as shown.

2. On each of the gameboards copy one group of problems in the manner shown in the illustration.

Group 1	Group 2	Group 3
14 − 7	15 − 9	11 − 7
12 − 3	14 − 6	13 − 8
21 − 6	23 − 5	22 − 6
28 − 9	21 − 8	24 − 7
33 − 5	35 − 8	31 − 5

3. Mark and cut the small posterboard pieces using the candy cane pattern shown here. Color red stripes on eight candy canes and green stripes on the other seven.

4. Copy each of the following numerals on a different red candy cane as shown in the illustration.

7, 6, 4, 9, 8, 5, 15, 18

5. Copy each of the following numerals on a different green candy cane as shown in the illustration.

16, 19, 13, 17, 28, 27, 26

6. Cut and glue the red and green construction paper to the spinner as shown here.

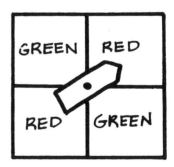

Game Play: This game may be played by two or three players.

1. Each player chooses a gameboard. The red candy canes are placed in one pile face down, and the green canes are placed face down in another pile in the center of the playing area.

2. The first player spins. He then picks up the top card from either the red or green stack, depending upon the spin.

3. He looks over the problems on his gameboard to find one to which his answer could be correctly matched. If he finds one, he places the cane on the appropriate candy jar. If not, he places the cane face down on the bottom of the same-color stack. The next player continues the game in the same manner.

4. The first player to correctly place a candy cane on each jar is the winner.

Ghost Game

Skill Reinforced: Double-digit subtrahend and double-digit minuend/Regrouping

Materials Needed:
■ 1 sheet of 12″ × 12″ white posterboard
■ 20 sheets of 3″ × 4″ white posterboard
■ scissors
■ game markers
■ felt-tipped pens in various colors
■ dice

Construction Directions:

1. Copy the gameboard shown here on the large sheet of posterboard.

2. Cut and mark the small posterboard pieces using the ghost pattern shown here.

3. Copy each of the following problems onto a different ghost as shown in the illustration.

21	32	43	57	61
−13	−14	−35	−49	−48
42	70	32	52	33
−29	−57	−19	−37	−18
40	21	38	44	56
−25	− 6	− 9	−15	−27
82	27	53	44	65
−53	− 9	−35	−26	−47

Game Play: This game may be played by two to four players.

1. Each player chooses a marker and places it on the gameboard making sure it is *not* on a ghost. All the ghosts are dealt to the players.

2. The first player rolls the dice and moves his marker the number of spaces indicated. The players take turns rolling the dice and moving the markers around the gameboard. When a player lands on a ghost, she looks through the ghosts in her hand to find one with a problem whose answer is that shown on the gameboard ghost. If she has one, she discards the ghost.

3. The players continue to move around the gameboard until one of them had discarded all his ghosts. This player is the winner.

Around the Zoo

Skill Reinforced: Single-digit divisor and double-digit dividend/No regrouping/No remainders/Basic facts

Materials Needed:
- 1 sheet of 12″ × 16″ white posterboard
- 32 sheets of 2½″ × 3″ yellow posterboard
- 4 game markers
- felt-tipped pens in various colors

Construction Directions:
1. Mark the white posterboard piece using an enlargement of the gameboard pattern shown here.

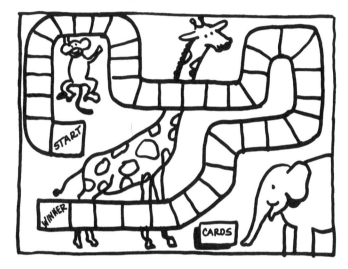

2. Copy each of the following sets of problems and directions onto a different yellow card.

$10 \div 2 =$
Move ahead one space.

$18 \div 9 =$
Move ahead two spaces.

$15 \div 5 =$
Move ahead three spaces.

$14 \div 7 =$
Move ahead one space.

$12 \div 2 =$
Move ahead two spaces.

$16 \div 4 =$
Move ahead three spaces.

$27 \div 9 =$
Move ahead one space.

$45 \div 9 =$
Move ahead two spaces.

$72 \div 9 =$
Move ahead three spaces.

$21 \div 3 =$
Move ahead one space.

$28 \div 7 =$
Move ahead two spaces.

$36 \div 4 =$
Move ahead three spaces.

$36 \div 6 =$
Move ahead one space.

$25 \div 5 =$
Move ahead two spaces.

$42 \div 7 =$
Move ahead three spaces.

$49 \div 7 =$
Move ahead one space.

$56 \div 7 =$
Move ahead two spaces.

$48 \div 8 =$
Move ahead three spaces.

$63 \div 7 =$
Move ahead three spaces.

$32 \div 8 =$
Move ahead one space.

$81 \div 9 =$
Move ahead two spaces.

$20 \div 4 =$
Move ahead three spaces.

$40 \div 8 =$
Move ahead one space.

$24 \div 3 =$
Move ahead two spaces.

$56 \div 8 =$
Move ahead three spaces.

Lion is loose.
Lose a turn.

Stop to watch monkeys.
Go back two spaces.

Feed the elephants.
Go back three spaces.

You are lost.
Go back one space.

You ate too much popcorn and got sick.
Go back three spaces.

Zoo is closed today.
Lose a turn.

Lost your money.
Go back two spaces.

Game Play: This game is for two to four players.
1. The gameboard is placed on a flat surface in the center of the group of players. All the cards should be shuffled and then stacked face down on the board where indicated. Each player chooses a marker and places it on "Start."
2. The first player takes the top card and reads the problem aloud. If he can correctly give the answer, he follows the directions on the card. If he is incorrect, he places the card face down on the bottom of the stack and the next player takes a turn. *Note:* A few cards are "penalty cards." When a player picks one of these, she simply follows the directions on the card.
3. The first player to reach the "Winner" space wins the game.

PART III

Puzzle Sheets

The puzzle sheets described in this part of the book lead students to the solutions of problems and equations in a unique and challenging way. The puzzles are, for the most part, self-checking, to give immediate feedback to both students and teachers. For those puzzles that are not self-checking, answer keys are included for quick and easy reference.

The puzzle sheets are grouped together at the back of the book so that they may be detached and duplicated with a minimum of time and effort. In this way, they may be put to use most conveniently as reinforcers of a variety of mathematical skills.

The Haunted Forest

Skill Reinforced: Sequencing 0–10

Puzzle Description: The children cut their sheets into strips along the broken lines and then place the strips in the correct numerical order. If they complete this task correctly, they will form a picture of a haunted forest. This puzzle sheet is on page 48.

Answer Key: The puzzle is self-correcting. The illustration shows a correctly completed haunted forest.

A Look into the Future

Skill Reinforced: Sequencing 1–29

Puzzle Description: The children begin at the star and draw a line to the number 1. They continue drawing lines from number to number in the correct sequence. If they complete the activity sheet correctly, the lines will form a picture. This puzzle sheet is on page 49.

Answer Key: The puzzle is self-correcting. As shown below, a picture of a space ship will be formed if the dots are connected in the correct order.

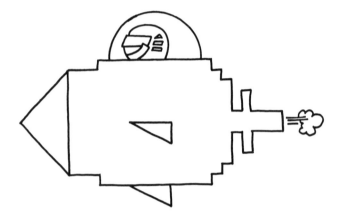

Fancy Flowers

Skill Reinforced: Commutative property/Zero as addend/Basic addition facts/Single-digit addends

Puzzle Description: The puzzle consists of a picture of flowers in a vase. Each flower has a problem on it. The children are to color only the flowers that have a problem whose sum is 5. After completing the puzzle, the children should be allowed to color in the entire picture. This puzzle sheet is on page 50.

Answer Key: This puzzle is easily evaluated. Simply check to see if each child has colored only those flowers with problems whose sum is 5. They are: $1 + 4$; $2 + 3$; $0 + 5$; $3 + 2$; $4 + 1$; $5 + 0$.

Name the Railroad

Skill Reinforced: Single-digit subtrahend, single-digit minuend/Basic subtraction facts

Puzzle Description: This puzzle consists of a drawing of a train and its path to a station. Along the way are outlines of nine boxcars. Inside each is a problem. At the bottom of the page are the "missing" boxcars, which have answers on them. The children cut out the boxcars and paste them over the appropriate problems. If they complete the puzzle correctly, the letters on the boxcars will spell the name of the railroad. This puzzle sheet may be found on page 51.

Answer Key: The puzzle is self-correcting. As shown below, the name NORTHWEST will appear if the puzzle is completed correctly.

N	2
O	8
R	9
T	7
H	5
W	4
E	6
S	1
T	3

In the Doghouse

Skill Reinforced: Multiplication fact families/ Commutative property

Puzzle Description: The children are asked to help each dog find his own doghouse. They must cut out the dog cards, each containing a problem, and paste them on the paths leading to their correct "answer" doghouse. This puzzle sheet is on page 52.

Answer Key: The puzzle is easily corrected. Simply check for the following problem/answer combinations.

12	*18*	*20*
1 × 12	1 × 18	2 × 10
4 × 3	2 × 9	4 × 5
3 × 4	9 × 2	5 × 4
12 × 1	18 × 1	10 × 2

Cindy Circle

Skill Reinforced: Recognition of operational symbols

Puzzle Description: The puzzle consists of one list of operations and another list of symbols. The students are to correctly match these by drawing a line from the symbol to the operation it represents and writing the circled letter in the space provided. This puzzle sheet may be found on page 53.

Answer Key: The puzzle is self-correcting. As shown below, the words DONUT SHAPE will be spelled if the puzzle is completed correctly.

D	ⓓivision
O	additiⓞn
N	ⓝot equal to
U	ⓤnion
T	equal ⓣo
S	interⓢection
H	greater tⓗan
A	subtr@ction
P	multiⓟlication
E	lⓔss than

Magic Squares

Skill Reinforced: Single- and double-digit addends/ Regrouping

Puzzle Description: The students are given instructions as to how to work through a magic square. In so doing they discover that the answer is always the same, whether they add vertically, horizontally, or from corner to corner. They are then told to work through three more squares to determine if they are also magic. This puzzle sheet is on page 54.

Answer Key: The puzzle is easily corrected. All squares are "magic," and so all should be circled.

Diver Dan

Skill Reinforced: Zero in subtraction/Double-digit minuend, double-digit subtrahend/Regrouping

Puzzle Description: The students follow the diver's path. Each time they come to a problem they copy down the correct answer and its corresponding letter from the treasure chest. If they are correct, the letters will spell what the diver found on the bottom of the sea. The puzzle is on page 55.

Answer Key: The puzzle is self-correcting. As shown below, the letters will spell the words IT IS SEAWEED if the student completes the puzzle correctly.

I	15
T	31
I	42
S	27
S	47
E	48
A	33
W	26
E	45
E	38
D	22

PART IV

Learning Boards

T his section of the book consists of display and bulletin board ideas that involve students in learning mathematics in an active way—a way that requires them to use more than just their visual sense. These boards not only encourage the development of specific mathematical skills or concepts but also create a high level of interest in the topic being studied.

Directions for constructing and using the boards are given in detail. All may be easily modified to fit the space available in any particular classroom.

The learning boards may be used to implement and/ or enrich the textbook materials, whether they are used for introductory, developmental, or reinforcement purposes.

Wash Day

Skill Reinforced: Ordinal numbers

Materials Needed:
- white background paper
- felt-tipped pens in various colors
- red construction paper
- posterboard in various colors
- paper clips
- white posterboard
- small Jell-O boxes
- stapler
- glue
- heavy string
- legal-size envelope
- scissors

Construction Directions:
1. Cut and mark the white posterboard using the tree patterns in the bulletin board illustration on page 78.
2. Staple the small boxes to the board and then glue the trees to these. This will give the trees a three-dimensional effect.
3. Tie the heavy string to the trees in the manner shown in the illustration.

4. Use the opaque projector and trace the figures and lettering onto the background paper.
5. Cut, mark, and attach a paper clip to the various-colored posterboards using the shirt pattern shown below.

PAPER CLIP

PUNCH HOLE

FIRST

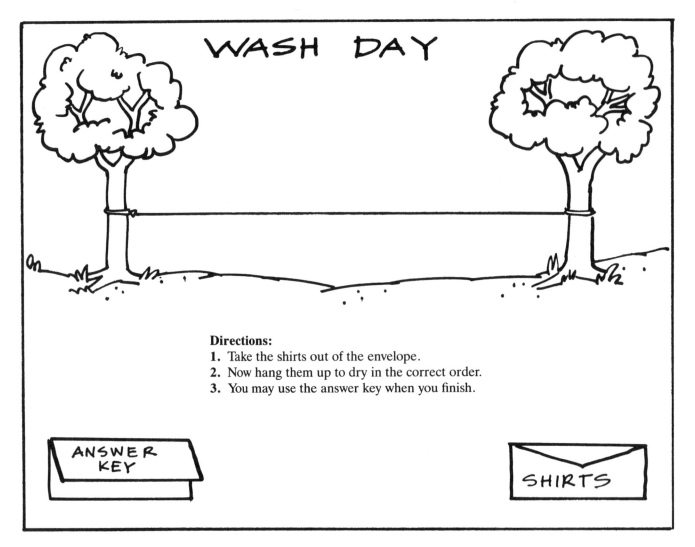

WASH DAY

Directions:
1. Take the shirts out of the envelope.
2. Now hang them up to dry in the correct order.
3. You may use the answer key when you finish.

ANSWER KEY

SHIRTS

6. Print each of the following words on a different shirt as shown in the illustration.

first	second	third
fourth	fifth	sixth
seventh	eighth	ninth
tenth		

7. Write "Shirts" on the envelope, attach it to the board, and place the shirts in it.

8. Fold the red construction paper and write "Answer Key" on the cover. Copy the following words onto the inside of the answer key and attach it to the board.

first
second
third
fourth
fifth
sixth
seventh
eighth
ninth
tenth

Learning Board Use: The children take the shirts out of the envelope and hang them on the clothesline in the correct ordinal positions. They may use the answer key when they finish.

Down the Rabbit Hole

Skill Reinforced: Basic addition facts/Number fact families

Materials Needed:
- white background paper
- 7 round potato chip cans
- white posterboard
- green Con-Tact paper
- thumbtacks
- scissors
- green construction paper
- legal-size envelope
- felt-tipped pens in various colors

From *Math Motivators*, Copyright © 1986 Scott, Foresman and Company

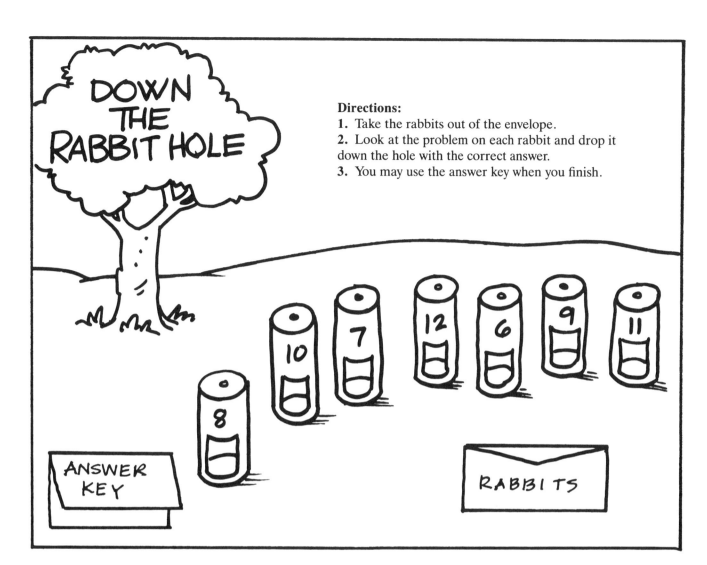

DOWN THE RABBIT HOLE

Directions:
1. Take the rabbits out of the envelope.
2. Look at the problem on each rabbit and drop it down the hole with the correct answer.
3. You may use the answer key when you finish.

ANSWER KEY

RABBITS

Construction Directions:
1. Use an opaque projector to trace the figures and lettering onto the background paper.
2. Cover the potato chip cans with the green Con-Tact paper and cut out part of the side as shown here.

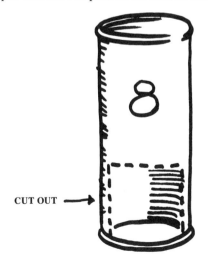

CUT OUT →

3. Copy each of the following numerals onto a different can and attach the cans to the board with thumbtacks as shown in the illustration.

8, 10, 7, 12, 6, 9, 11

4. Cut and mark the white posterboard using the following rabbit pattern. You will need 28 rabbits.

---

5. Copy each of the following problems onto a different rabbit as shown in the illustration.

4 + 4 =	3 + 7 =	6 + 1 =
1 + 7 =	5 + 5 =	2 + 5 =
3 + 5 =	10 + 0 =	3 + 4 =
2 + 6 =	4 + 6 =	0 + 7 =
6 + 6 =	3 + 3 =	0 + 9 =
5 + 7 =	0 + 6 =	1 + 8 =
4 + 8 =	5 + 1 =	2 + 7 =
12 + 0 =	2 + 4 =	3 + 6 =
10 + 1 =	9 + 2 =	11 + 0 =
3 + 8 =		

6. Write "Rabbits" on the large envelope, attach it to the board, and place the rabbits in it.

7. Fold the green construction paper and write "Answer Key" on the cover. Copy the following problems onto the inside of the answer key and attach it to the board.

8	10	7
1 + 7 =	3 + 7 =	6 + 1 =
4 + 4 =	5 + 5 =	2 + 5 =
3 + 5 =	10 + 0 =	3 + 4 =
2 + 6 =	4 + 6 =	0 + 7 =
12	**6**	**9**
6 + 6 =	3 + 3 =	0 + 9 =
5 + 7 =	0 + 6 =	1 + 8 =
4 + 8 =	5 + 1 =	2 + 7 =
12 + 0 =	2 + 4 =	3 + 6 =
11		
10 + 1 =		
9 + 2 =		
11 + 0 =		
3 + 8 =		

Learning Board Use: The children take the rabbits out of the envelope and match the problems on the rabbits to the answers on the rabbit holes by dropping the rabbits down the holes. They may use the answer key when they finish.

The Lickity Pickity Fence

Skill Reinforced: Three single-digit addends/Sums less than 10

Materials Needed:
- white background paper
- white posterboard
- felt-tipped pens in various colors
- straight pins
- scissors
- paper hole punch
- white construction paper
- legal-size envelope
- stapler

Construction Directions:

1. Use an opaque projector to trace the fence and lettering onto the background paper. Use appropriate colors.

2. Attach the straight pins over the picket fence as shown in the illustration.

3. Cut, punch, and mark the posterboard using the cat pattern shown here.

PUNCH HOLE

4. Copy each of the following numbers onto a different cat as shown.

3, 4, 5, 6, 7, 8, 9

5. Write "Cats" on the envelope, attach it to the board, and place all the cats in it.

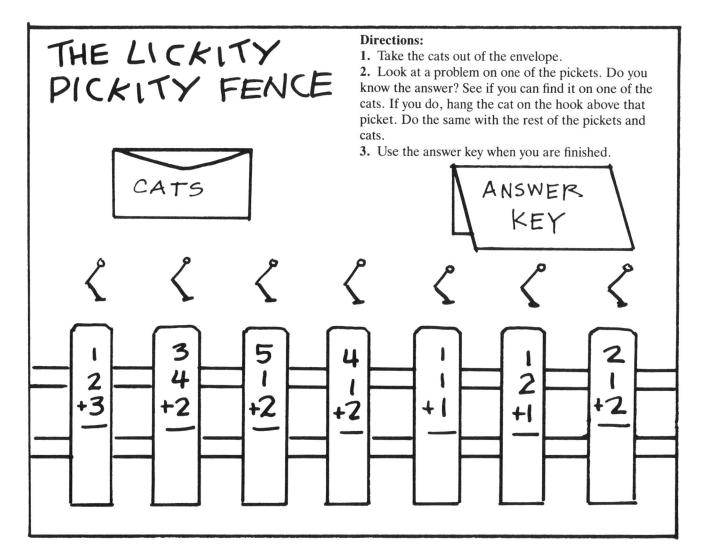

Directions:
1. Take the cats out of the envelope.
2. Look at a problem on one of the pickets. Do you know the answer? See if you can find it on one of the cats. If you do, hang the cat on the hook above that picket. Do the same with the rest of the pickets and cats.
3. Use the answer key when you are finished.

CATS

ANSWER KEY

Pickets:
$$\begin{array}{r} 1 \\ 2 \\ +3 \\ \hline \end{array} \quad \begin{array}{r} 3 \\ 4 \\ +2 \\ \hline \end{array} \quad \begin{array}{r} 5 \\ 1 \\ +2 \\ \hline \end{array} \quad \begin{array}{r} 4 \\ 1 \\ +2 \\ \hline \end{array} \quad \begin{array}{r} 1 \\ 1 \\ +1 \\ \hline \end{array} \quad \begin{array}{r} 1 \\ 2 \\ +1 \\ \hline \end{array} \quad \begin{array}{r} 2 \\ 1 \\ +2 \\ \hline \end{array}$$

6. Fold the construction paper to form an answer key and mark the front as shown in the board illustration. Copy the following problems onto the inside of the answer key.

$$1 + 2 + 3 = 6$$
$$3 + 4 + 2 = 9$$
$$5 + 1 + 2 = 8$$
$$4 + 1 + 2 = 7$$
$$1 + 1 + 1 = 3$$
$$1 + 2 + 1 = 4$$
$$2 + 1 + 2 = 5$$

Learning Board Use: Children take the cats out of the envelope and hang the correct answers over the problems on each picket. When they are finished, they may use the answer key to check themselves.

Subtraction Spin

Skill Reinforced: Basic subtraction facts

Materials Needed:
- yellow background paper
- large sheet of black posterboard
- 9 sheets of white construction paper
- felt-tipped pens in various colors
- scissors
- long thumbtack
- 9 small Jell-O boxes
- stapler
- glue

Construction Directions:
1. Use an opaque projector to trace the number sheet and lettering onto the background paper.
2. Cut out a spinner arrow from the black posterboard and attach it to the learning board with a long thumbtack.

Subtraction Spin

Directions:
1. Twirl the spinner.
2. When it stops on a numeral, find a problem with that answer.
3. When you finish, check the answer key.

Spinner numerals: 3 8 2 4 7 5 0 6 1

Tops: 9-1=   4-4=   8-6=   7-2=   8-1=   7-3=   9-3=   7-6=   6-3=

ANSWER KEY

---

3. Cut and mark the white construction paper using the top pattern shown here.

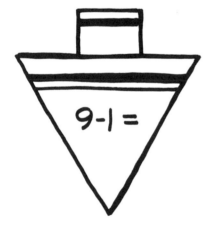

9-1 =

4. Copy each of the following problems onto a different top as shown in the illustration.

$$9 - 1 = \qquad 4 - 4 =$$
$$7 - 2 = \qquad 8 - 1 =$$
$$6 - 3 = \qquad 8 - 6 =$$
$$7 - 3 = \qquad 9 - 3 =$$
$$7 - 6 =$$

5. Attach the small Jell-O boxes to the board and glue the tops to these. This will give a three-dimensional effect.

6. Fold a sheet of white construction paper to form an answer key and mark the front cover as shown. Write the following problems on the inside and attach to the board.

$$9 - 1 = 8 \qquad 4 - 4 = 0$$
$$7 - 2 = 5 \qquad 8 - 1 = 7$$
$$6 - 3 = 3 \qquad 8 - 6 = 2$$
$$7 - 3 = 4 \qquad 9 - 3 = 6$$
$$7 - 6 = 1$$

Learning Board Use: Children spin the arrow. When it stops on a numeral, they must find the top whose answer is the same as that numeral. When they finish, they may use the answer key to correct themselves.

TURTLE MANIA

Directions:
1. Look at one of the turtles. Do you know what the missing symbol is?
2. When you think you know, fold down the turtle's shell to see if you are correct.

Turtle Mania

Skill Reinforced: Number sentences/Recognition of operation symbols

Materials Needed:
- white background paper
- felt-tipped pens in various colors
- green construction paper
- scissors
- stapler

Construction Directions:
1. Use an opaque projector to trace the figures and lettering onto the background paper.
2. Cut, mark, and attach the green construction paper using the turtle pattern shown here. You will need ten turtles.
3. Copy each of the following number sentences onto a different turtle as shown in the illustration. Copy the missing symbol (in parentheses) under the top of the turtle's shell.

$$9 \ \square \ 5 = 4 \ (-)$$
$$6 \ \square \ 4 = 24 \ (\times)$$
$$25 \div 5 \ \square \ 5 \ (=)$$
$$16 \ \square \ 12 = 28 \ (+)$$
$$14 \ \square \ 7 = 2 \ (\div)$$
$$2 \ \square \ 1 = 2 \ (\div)$$
$$20 \ \square \ 10 = 10 \ (-)$$
$$4 \ \square \ 3 = 12 \ (\times)$$
$$35 \ \square \ 15 = 20 \ (-)$$
$$22 \ \square \ 27 = 49 \ (+)$$

Learning Board Use: Children are to figure out the missing symbol on each turtle. When they think they know, they fold down the turtle's shell to view the correct answer.

FOLD

$9 \ \square \ 5 = 4$

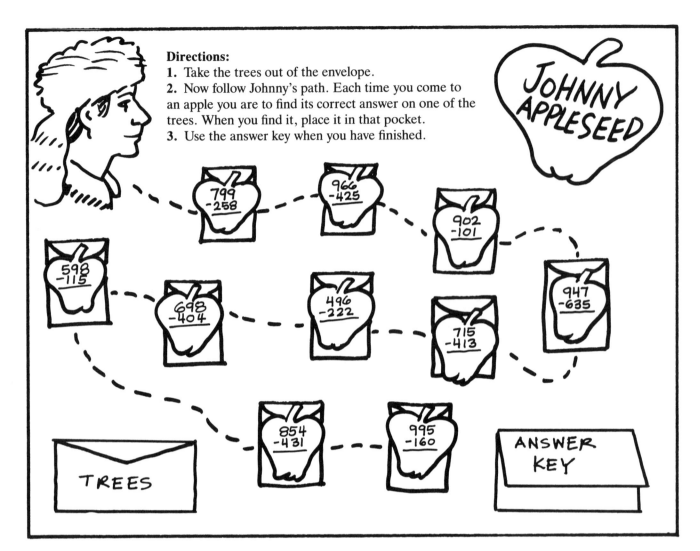

Directions:
1. Take the trees out of the envelope.
2. Now follow Johnny's path. Each time you come to an apple you are to find its correct answer on one of the trees. When you find it, place it in that pocket.
3. Use the answer key when you have finished.

Johnny Appleseed

Skill Reinforced: Multidigit subtrahend and multidigit minuend/No regrouping

Materials Needed:
- white background paper
- felt-tipped pens in various colors
- red construction paper
- green construction paper
- 10 library-book card pockets
- legal-size envelope
- scissors
- glue
- stapler

Construction Directions:
1. Use an opaque projector to trace the figures and lettering onto the background paper as shown in the illustration above.

2. Cut and mark the red construction paper using the apple pattern shown here.

3. Glue the apples to the library-book card pockets and attach them to the board.

4. Copy each of the following problems onto a different apple as shown in the illustration.

799	866	902	947	715
-258	-425	-101	-635	-413

496	698	854	598	995
-222	-404	-431	-115	-160

5. Cut and mark the green posterboard using the tree pattern shown here.

6. Copy each of the following answers onto a different tree.

541, 441, 801, 312, 302, 274, 294, 423, 483, 835

7. Attach the large envelope to the board and place the trees in it.

8. Fold a sheet of the red construction paper and mark the cover as shown in the illustration.

9. Write the following problems inside the answer key and attach it to the board.

799	866	902	947	715
-258	-425	-101	-635	-413
541	441	801	312	302

496	698	854	598	995
-222	-404	-431	-115	-160
274	294	423	483	835

Learning Board Use: Children take the trees out of the envelope and follow Johnny Appleseed's path. Each time they come to an apple they are to find the correct answer on one of the trees and put the tree into that pocket. When they finish, they may use the answer key.

Directions:

1. Take the umbrellas out of the envelope.
2. Match the umbrellas to the sets of raindrops by placing the correct umbrella into the ducks' pockets.
3. When you are finished, use the answer key to check yourself.

Looks Like Rain

Skill Reinforced: Single-digit multiplicand and single-digit multiplier

Materials Needed:
- blue background paper
- red posterboard
- cotton batting
- black construction paper
- straight pins
- library-book card pockets
- gray construction paper
- yellow construction paper
- felt-tipped pen
- legal-size envelope
- stapler
- glue

Construction Directions:
1. Cut and attach the cotton batting to form the title cloud.
2. Cut the black construction paper using the letter patterns below and attach them to the cotton cloud with the straight pins.

3. Use an opaque projector to trace the rain drops and lettering onto the background paper.
4. Cut and mark the yellow construction paper using the duck pattern shown below.

36　LEARNING BOARDS

5. Glue the ducks to the library-book card pockets and attach them to the board as shown in the illustration.

6. Cut and mark the red posterboard using the umbrella pattern shown here.

5 sets of 4

7. Copy each of the following onto a different umbrella as shown in the illustration.

> 5 sets of 4
> 3 sets of 3
> 4 sets of 2
> 3 sets of 6
> 2 sets of 5
> 5 sets of 3
> 2 sets of 3
> 6 sets of 2

8. Write the word "Umbrellas" on the large envelope, attach it to the board, and place the umbrellas in it.

9. Fold the gray construction paper to form an answer key and mark the front as shown in the board illustration. Copy the following onto the inside of the answer key and attach it to the board.

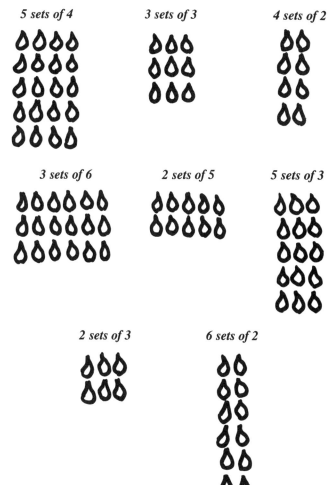

5 sets of 4 *3 sets of 3* *4 sets of 2*

3 sets of 6 *2 sets of 5* *5 sets of 3*

2 sets of 3 *6 sets of 2*

Learning Board Use: Children take the umbrellas out of the envelope and match them to the raindrops by placing the umbrellas in the appropriate duck pockets. When they finish, they may use the answer key to correct themselves.

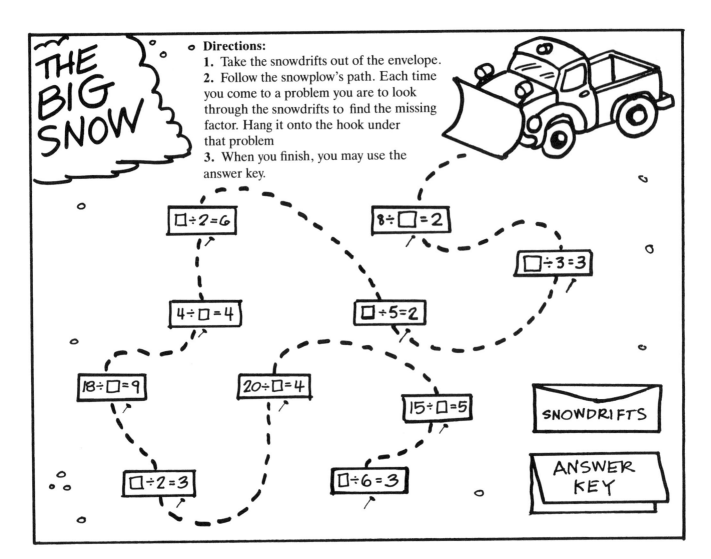

The Big Snow

Skill Reinforced: Basic division facts

Materials Needed:
- white background paper
- white posterboard
- felt-tipped pens in various colors
- straight pins
- scissors
- paper hole punch
- blue construction paper
- legal-size envelope
- stapler

Construction Directions:

1. Use an opaque projector to trace the figures and lettering onto the background paper.
2. Attach the straight pins as shown in the illustration.
3. Cut, mark, and punch the posterboard using the following snowdrift pattern.

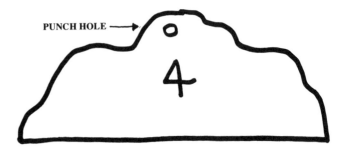

PUNCH HOLE →

4. Copy each of the following numerals onto a different snowdrift as shown in the illustration.

4, 9, 10, 12, 1, 2, 6, 5, 3, 18

5. Print "Snowdrifts" on the envelope, attach it to the board, and place the snowdrifts inside.

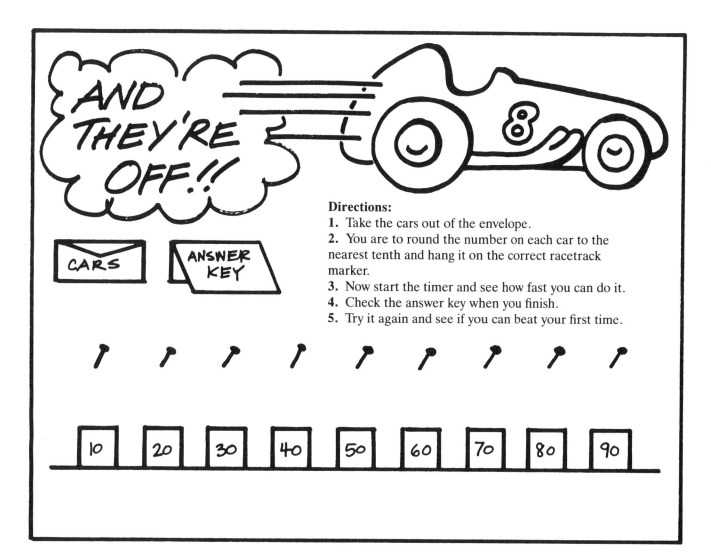

Directions:
1. Take the cars out of the envelope.
2. You are to round the number on each car to the nearest tenth and hang it on the correct racetrack marker.
3. Now start the timer and see how fast you can do it.
4. Check the answer key when you finish.
5. Try it again and see if you can beat your first time.

6. Fold the blue construction paper to form an answer key and mark the cover as shown in the illustration. Write the following problems on the inside and attach the answer key to the board.

$$8 \div 4 = 2 \qquad 9 \div 3 = 3$$
$$10 \div 5 = 2 \qquad 12 \div 2 = 6$$
$$4 \div 1 = 4 \qquad 18 \div 2 = 9$$
$$6 \div 2 = 3 \qquad 20 \div 5 = 4$$
$$15 \div 3 = 5 \qquad 18 \div 6 = 3$$

Learning Board Use: Children take the snowdrifts out of the envelope and follow the snowplow's path. Each time they come to a problem they look for the missing factor on one of the snowdrifts. When they find it, they hang it on the hook under the problem. They may use the answer key when they finish.

And They're Off!

Skill Reinforced: Rounding two-digit numbers

Materials Needed:
- white background paper
- felt-tipped pens in various colors
- posterboard in various colors
- straight pins
- gray construction paper
- small Jell-O boxes
- legal-size envelope
- scissors
- stapler
- timer

Construction Directions:
1. Use an opaque projector to trace and cut the title/exhaust cloud from the gray construction paper. Attach the small Jell-O boxes to the board and glue the cloud to these. This will give a three-dimensional effect.
2. Use an opaque projector to trace the figures and lettering onto the background paper. Attach the straight pins as shown.

3. Cut, mark, and punch the posterboard using the racing car pattern shown below. You will need 18 cars.

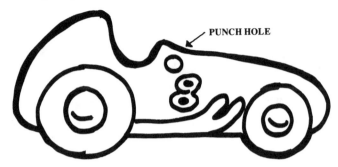

PUNCH HOLE

4. Copy each of the following numbers onto a different car.

8, 13, 18, 24, 26, 33, 36, 41, 47, 52, 56, 63
67, 74, 78, 82, 86, 91

5. Mark the word "Cars" on the envelope, attach it to the board, and place the cars in it.

6. Fold the gray construction paper to form an answer key and mark the front cover as shown in the board illustration. Copy the following lists on the inside of the answer key.

Race Markers	Correct Cars
10	8, 13
20	18, 24
30	26, 33
40	36, 41
50	47, 52
60	56, 63
70	67, 74
80	78, 82
90	86, 91

7. Place the timer near the learning board.

Learning Board Use: Students take the cars out of the envelope. They start the timer and "race" across the track by rounding the numbers on the cars to the nearest tenth and hanging them on the appropriate track markers. When they finish, they may use the answer key to correct themselves. They may want to do the activity again to try to beat their first time.

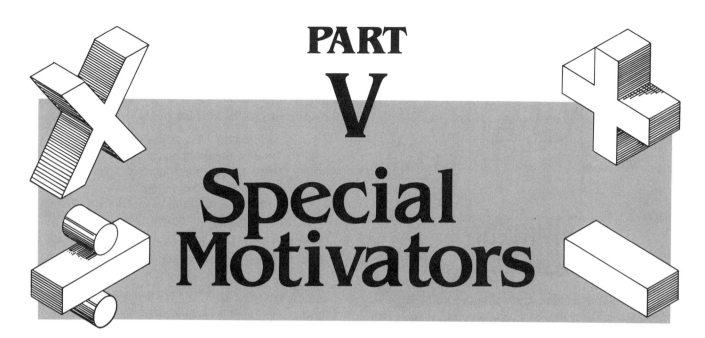

PART
V
Special Motivators

$\mathbf{A}$lthough this entire book is designed to provide motivational activities for students, this section contains some special kinds of motivators. It includes, for example, the idea of private "nooks" and interest centers to which students can retreat to do work. There are also directions for making delightfully original bookmarks, which will encourage a high and constant level of effort, and for making puppets that will attract and hold students' attention.

The versatility of the motivators permits them to be easily adapted for other grade levels, with variations made at the discretion of the teacher.

Have a Whale of a Good Time!

You can make an irresistible math nook with the help of a large cardboard box (refrigerator boxes are a perfect size), a razor knife, felt-tipped pens, and tape. Simply turn the box on its side and then cut and assemble as shown here. Throw in a few pillows, add books and magazines about math, and watch the children take turns "being swallowed by the whale!"

IMPORTANT: Be sure to tape the back side of the nook to the wall for stability.

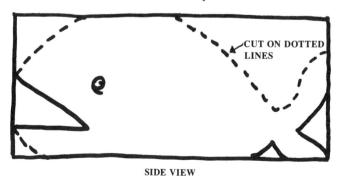

SIDE VIEW

| DISCARD | TOP OF WHALE | CUT ON DOTTED LINES DISCARD |

TOP VIEW

Melvin Moth's Math Club

Encourage your students to join Melvin Moth's Math Club, whereby they pledge to do all their math homework/classwork. Upon joining the math club, they receive a bookmark, as shown on the next page, and a Melvin Moth pledge sheet, as shown on page 56.

SUGGESTION: Copy the bookmark on a ditto master and run off copies using construction paper. The children can cut them out and color them.

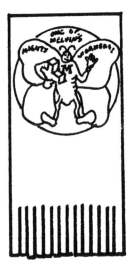

Every child who successfully completes a Melvin Moth pledge sheet should receive a button to wear like the one shown here. It can be easily made out of construction paper and pinned to the hard workers.

PIPE CLEANERS MAY BE TAPED TO THE BACKSIDE OF THE BUTTONS FOR ADDED APPEAL

You might want to continue club membership for another three-week period. The reward for all club members in good standing this time might be a Melvin Moth Munchie. This could be candy, cookies, or so on. If possible, a homemade cookie cut in the shape of a moth (or butterfly) would be perfect!

Mathematical Menagerie

Capitalize on children's attraction to animals by establishing a "mathematical menagerie" of puppets. The puppets named below can be made easily by following the directions on the next few pages.

> Mildred the Metric Mouse
> Freddie the Fraction Frog
> Samantha the Subtraction Snake
> Alfonse the Addition Ant
> Melody the Multiplication Monkey
> Dandelion the Division Dog

NOTE: These puppets can be used to attract and hold students' attention when introducing a new math topic or reviewing one that has already been presented.

Use a green sock to make Samantha. Cut out the eyes from white construction paper and the mouth from red posterboard. Glue the eyes onto the sock as shown and the mouth parts to the sole and heel like this.

Now mark the nose with a black felt-tipped pen and Samantha is ready for use.

To make Alfonse, use three small plastic foam balls, and color them with a gray felt-tipped pen. Now join them together with toothpicks. Use pipe cleaners for antennae and legs. Mark the eyes and mouth using a black felt-tipped pen. Finish the puppet by inserting a straightened piece of coat hanger into the bottom of the middle ball so Alfonse can be held up in front of the class.

Use a small gelatin or pudding box to make Mildred. Cover the box with gray Con-Tact paper, leaving one end open, and cut a small arc out of the bottom of the box that is big enough for your hand to fit through. Also cut five small finger holes in the bottom. Now cut the ears out of gray construction paper and attach them to the top of the box. Push six black pipe cleaners through the front of the box for whiskers. Draw the eyes, nose, and mouth with a black felt-tipped pen.

Freddie can be made from a large paper plate that is folded in half and painted green. Staple two soft margarine cups to the top of the plate for eyes, and cut a tongue from red construction paper.

Melody and Dandelion both require flat-ended paper sacks. Use colored construction paper to cut the eyes, ears, and nose, and fill in the details with felt-tipped pens.

Hip-Hip-Hooray for Math

Make this button out of construction paper and pin it on those who do well on their math assignments.

Mathmarks

Children love to use unusual bookmarks. Why not provide them with "mathmarks" for their math books?

NOTE: You might want to put sample "mathmarks" on a poster and have the children make their own!

Math just knocks me out!

I "vant" to do a problem.

No "lion" . . . I just love MATH!

I'm just "buggy" about math!

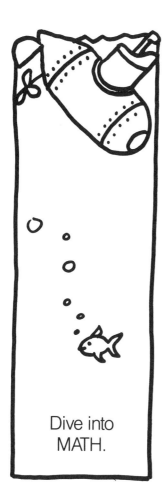

Dive into
MATH.

Have a
ball . . .
do some
MATH!

Go Fishing

Take your class "fishing" for their new math problems. All you need are a small wooden stick (a yardstick works well), a piece of string, a small horseshoe magnet, and several paper clips. Simply cut and mark small sheets of lightweight posterboard in the shape of the fish pattern shown here.

HOLE FOR
PAPER CLIP

Construct one fish for each problem. Print each problem on the backside of a fish and attach a paper clip to the mouth as shown. Now tie the string to one end of the stick, attach the magnet to the loose end of the string, and you are ready to go fishing!

Have the children arrange themselves in a circle and then place the fish on the floor in the center. Now let the children take turns fishing for problems. Once a fish is hooked, you read the problem on the back. If the child cannot give the correct answer, the fish will have to be thrown back! See who can catch the most fish.

Tic-Tac-Toe

Before beginning your math lesson, print each of the current problems both on a 4″ × 4″ card and on a round card that is 4″ in diameter. Put small pieces of double-stick tape on the backs of the cards and spread them across the chalk tray or floor so that the problems are face down.

Using masking tape or chalk, mark the chalkboard with a tic-tac-toe grid. Be sure that each space in the grid is large enough to contain a problem card.

Now you are ready to reinforce the math skill by playing tic-tac-toe. Divide your class into two teams for this activity. One team will use the square problem cards, and the other team will play with the round ones. Choose a team to go first. You might also choose two captains to decide the order in which the team members will participate.

The first player chooses a problem card from his team's pile of cards. He hands it to you without looking at the problem. You read the problem aloud and he must answer it correctly. If he does, he may stick the problem card onto one of the squares on the tic-tac-toe board. A child from the other team then chooses a problem card from her team's pile of cards, and the game continues. Each team must try to place three problem cards in a row. The row may be vertical, horizontal, or diagonal. If a child chooses a problem card and cannot answer it, he replaces the card in the team's pile and the team loses a turn.

Crossing the Amazon

Your students have a problem . . . they are on one side of the Amazon River and must get on the other side! They cannot swim across because of the alligators and hungry piranha fish. The only way to get across is to walk from one steppingstone to another. But the students must be careful not to slip and fall into the river!

Tell your students to pretend that the Amazon River flows across the classroom. Cut out odd-shaped "steppingstones" from construction paper. Choose a volun-

teer to attempt to cross the Amazon. She must correctly answer a problem for each stone she steps on. If she misses one of the problems, she falls into the water and must sit down until all the other children have had a turn. See how many children can cross the river—problem by problem—on their first try. Those who fall in the river may, of course, try again later.

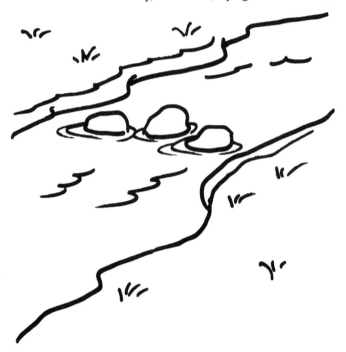

Worksheets

THE HAUNTED FOREST

Name _____

Date

Cut apart on dotted lines and put
back together in correct numerical order.

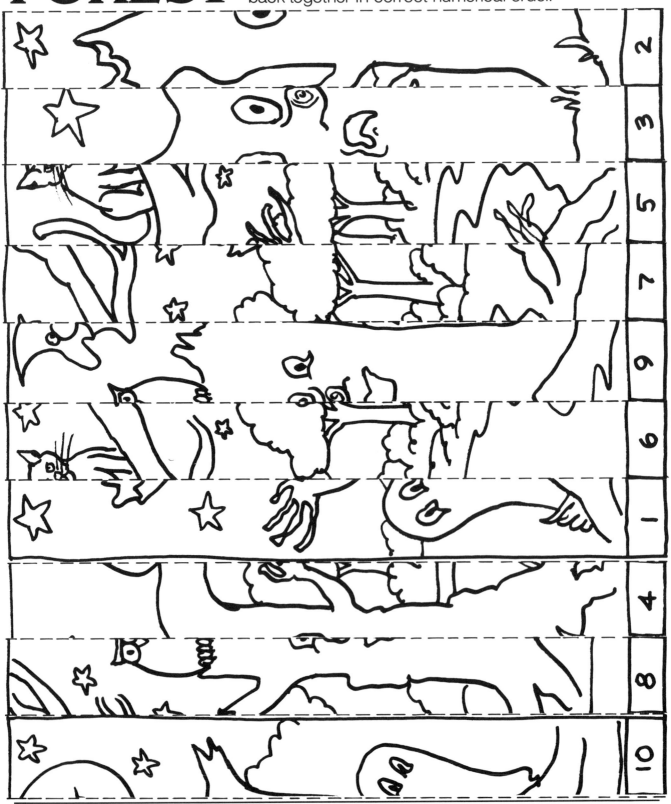

From *Math Motivators*, Copyright © 1986 Scott, Foresman and Company

A LOOK INTO THE FUTURE

Name _____

Date _____

Begin at the star and draw a line to the number 1. Keep drawing lines following the numerical order until you reach number 29.

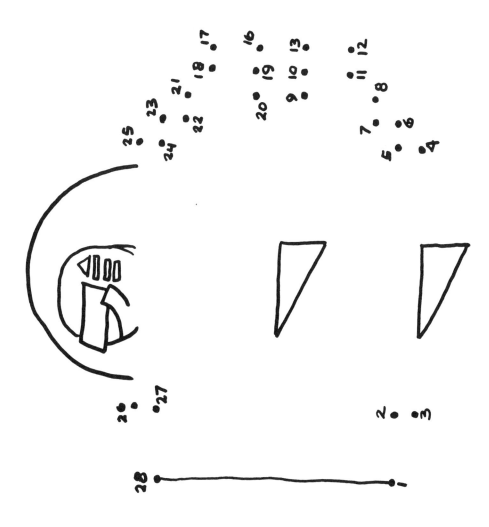

FANCY FLOWERS

Color only those flowers whose problem has a sum of 5.

Name _____

Date _____

NAME THE RAILROAD

Name _____

Date _____

Cut out the boxcars at the bottom of this page. Now follow the train tracks beginning at the engine. Each time you come to the outline of a boxcar, paste the boxcar with the correct answer over that problem. If you complete the puzzle correctly, the letters will spell the name of this railroad.

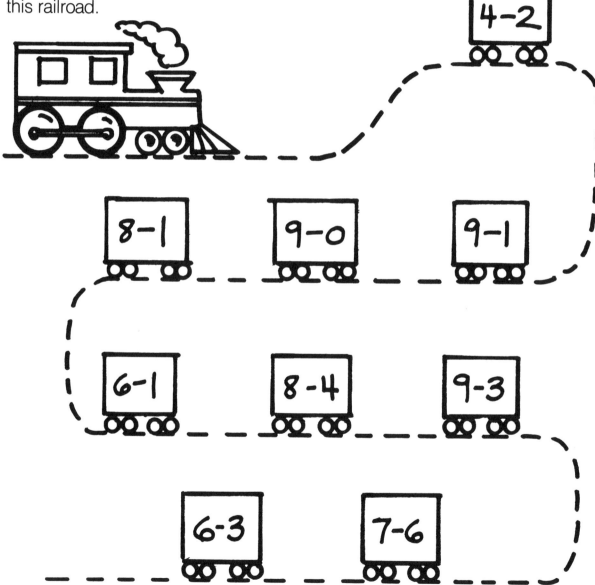

| 8O | 5H | 3T | 4W | 2N | 6E | 9R | 7T | 1S |

IN THE
DOGHOUSE

Name

Date

Help the dogs find their way to the right doghouse. Cut them out and paste them on a path that will take them home.

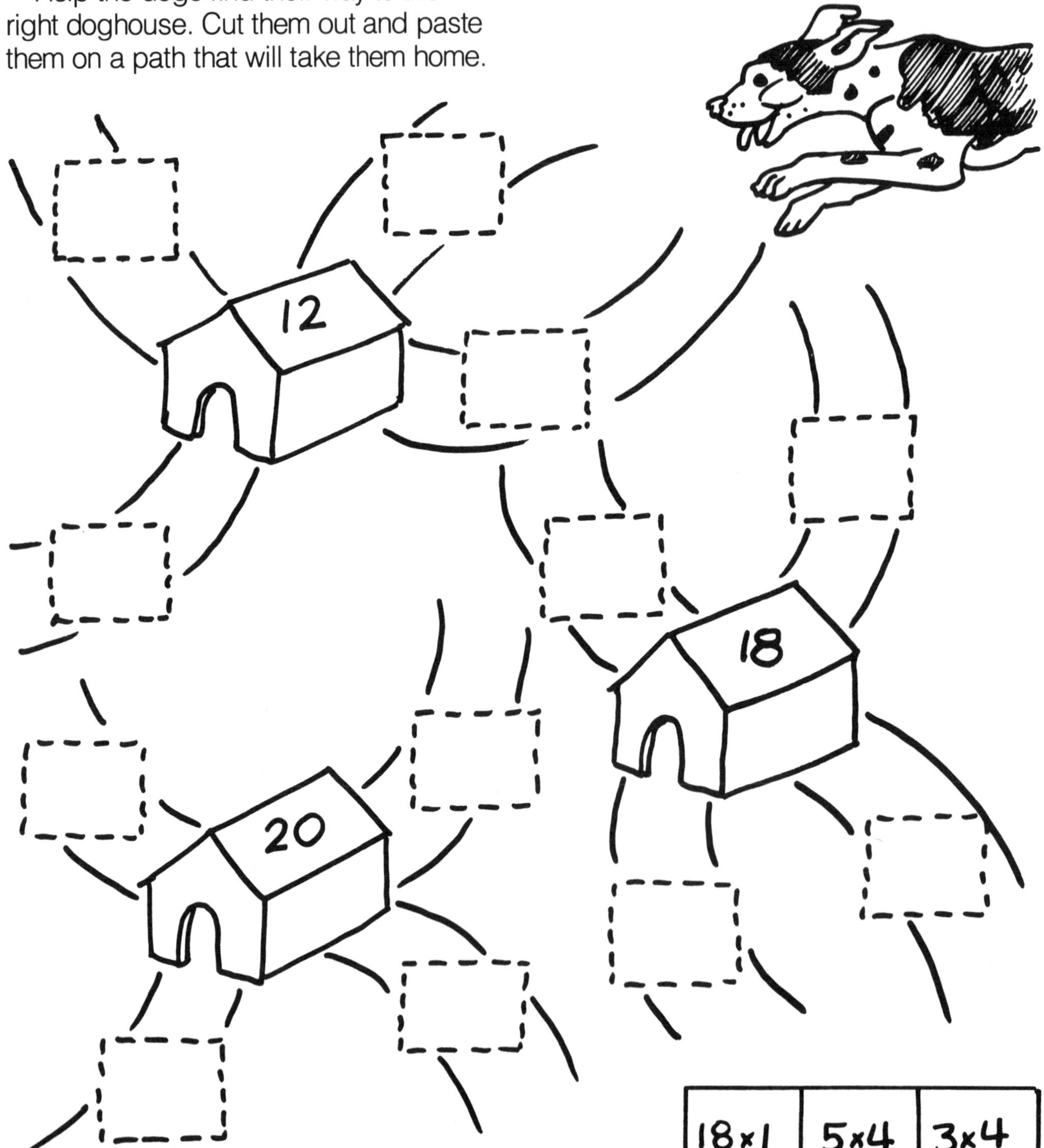

18×1	5×4	3×4

1×12	1×18	2×10	4×3	4×5	2×9	9×2	12×1	10×2

52 WORKSHEETS

From *Math Motivators,* Copyright © 1986 Scott, Foresman and Company

CINDY CIRCLE

Cindy Circle is shaped like something good to eat. If you can match the symbols to the operations they stand for, the circled letters will spell what shape Cindy is in. Simply draw a line from each symbol to its correct operation. Then write the circled letters in the spaces next to each symbol.

Name _____

Date _____

_____	÷	additi(o)n
_____	+	subtr(a)ction
_____	≠	multi(p)lication
_____	∩	(d)ivision
_____	=	equal (t)o
_____	∪	(n)ot equal to
_____	>	l(e)ss than
_____	−	greater t(h)an
_____	×	(u)nion
_____	<	inter(s)ection

From *Math Motivators,* Copyright © 1986 Scott, Foresman and Company

MAGIC SQUARES

Here is a magic square. Look at it carefully.

9	1	8
5	6	7
4	11	3

20	90	40
70	50	30
60	10	80

Do you see what's magic about it? Complete the following steps in order to find out.

1. Add the numbers in each row.
2. Add the numbers in each column.
3. Add the numbers from corner to corner.

Now do you know what the magic is? Sure . . . they all add up to the same number . . . 18. That's the magic!

Now do the same thing with the squares below and decide if they are magic too. Circle the ones you think are magic.

16	2	3	13
5	11	10	8
9	7	6	12
4	14	15	1

4	9	2
3	5	7
8	1	6

From *Math Motivators,* Copyright © 1986 Scott, Foresman and Company

DIVER DAN

Name _____

Date _____

Diver Dan has found something on the bottom of the sea. Help him bring it up to his boat. As you follow his path to the boat, complete each problem along the way. Look at the treasure chest and copy down the correct answer and letter next to it in the space under each problem. If you get all the answers right, the letters will spell what Diver Dan has found.

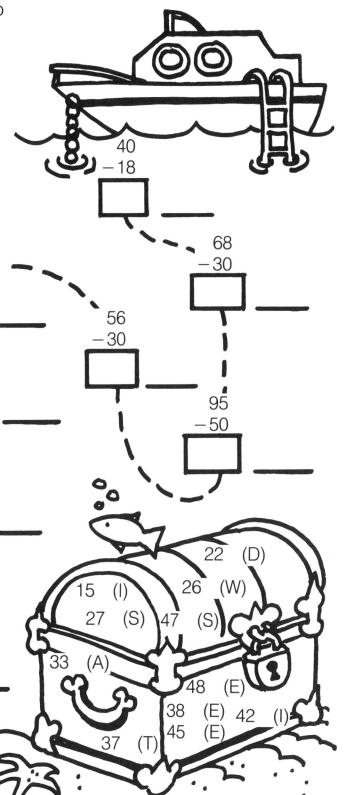

$$40 - 18$$

$$80 - 33$$

$$60 - 27$$

$$68 - 30$$

$$37 - 10$$

$$78 - 30$$

$$56 - 30$$

$$72 - 30$$

$$95 - 50$$

$$56 - 19$$

$$30 - 15$$

15   (I)
22   (D)
26   (W)
27   (S)   47   (S)
33   (A)
48   (E)
38   (E)   42   (I)
45   (E)
37   (T)

BE ONE OF MELVIN'S MIGHTY WORKERS

I, _____ ,
   (your name)
pledge to complete all my math
homework and classwork for the next
three weeks.

		Turned in	Handed back	Grade/score
First Week	Monday	_____	_____	_____
	Tuesday	_____	_____	_____
	Wednesday	_____	_____	_____
	Thursday	_____	_____	_____
	Friday	_____	_____	_____
Second Week	Monday	_____	_____	_____
	Tuesday	_____	_____	_____
	Wednesday	_____	_____	_____
	Thursday	_____	_____	_____
	Friday	_____	_____	_____
Third Week	Monday	_____	_____	_____
	Tuesday	_____	_____	_____
	Wednesday	_____	_____	_____
	Thursday	_____	_____	_____
	Friday	_____	_____	_____